SNAP SHOT™

Senior Editor Mary Ling
Art Editor Joanna Pocock
Editor Caroline Bingham
Designer Jane Thomas
Production Catherine Semark

A Dorling Kindersley Book
First published in Great Britain in 1994
by Snapshot™, an imprint of Covent Garden Books
9 Henrietta Street, London WC2E 8PS
2 4 6 8 10 9 7 5 3

A CIP catalogue record for this book is
available from the British Library
ISBN 1-85948-023-3

Colour reproduction by Colourscan
Printed in Belgium by Proost

Visit us on the World Wide Web at
http://www.dk.com

In the Sea

Contents

Sea lions

Can you swim like a fish?

Most of us can swim, and we can all
enjoy water when we're in a boat.
But unlike fish, if we want to explore
the underwater world, we need
tanks of special air to breathe.

How do whales breathe?

A whale breathes through a blowhole in its head. It has to rise to the surface of the sea to take each breath of air.

What a splash!

Dolphins love to play. Watch out for them as they splash and jump in the waves next to a boat.

9

A blanket of blubber

keeps out the cold

Walruses have an extra thick layer
of fat called blubber under their skin.
This keeps them warm in icy waters.

Colour ...

colour everywhere

A coral reef is a world
of bright colours and
crazy patterns. Watch
the tropical fish,
darting through
the water.

Seahorses cling to coral with their curly tails when they want to stop for a rest.

What

Many sea creatures have unusual shapes. Just look at this sea-urchin and sea-cucumber!

strange creatures!

Stars in the pool,

Look in a rockpool
by the sea and you
will find all sorts of
starfish and shells.

shells on the beach!

Pincer power!

Lobsters use their
huge pincers for
cutting and crushing
their food.

How does a crab walk?

This crab has six legs and a pair of pincers. It moves quickly, scuttling along sideways.

A snappy fisher!

Cormorants swoop into the sea to catch fish in their hooked bills.

What noisy birds!

Seagulls have a piercing cry as they hover overhead, looking for scraps.

Four fast swimmers!

These fish are all perfectly shaped for speeding through cool waters. Their silvery colours help them hunt and hide.

What do these boats do?

Tough little tug boats pull and push great big ships through tricky waterways and harbours.

Fishing trawlers head out to
sea to catch fish in huge nets.

Rescue me at sea!

R.N.L.I. ROYAL SHIPWRIGHT

12-004

Lifeboats rescue people from stormy seas. The rescuers wear lifejackets to help them stay afloat if they fall overboard. You should always wear a lifejacket.

Wind in the sails

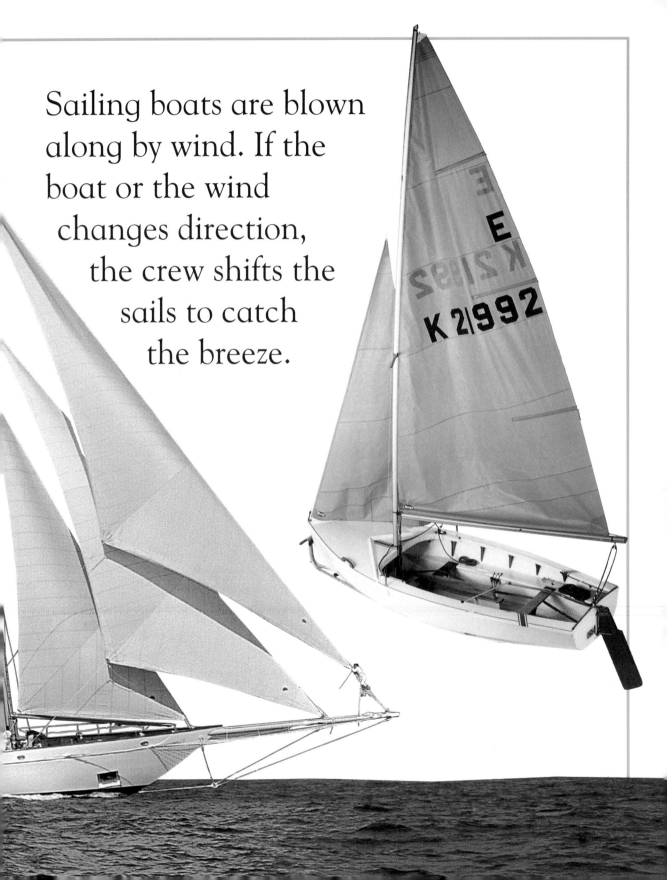

Sailing boats are blown along by wind. If the boat or the wind changes direction, the crew shifts the sails to catch the breeze.

1. Spiny boxfish

Guess the

3. Angel-fish

4. Starfish

2. Cowfish

sea shapes!

6. Stingray

5. Sea-urchin

Answers on page 32

Answers

1. Square
2. Rectangle
3. Triangle
4. Star
5. Circle
6. Diamond